MEDITATIONS BEFORE THE WINDOWS FAIL

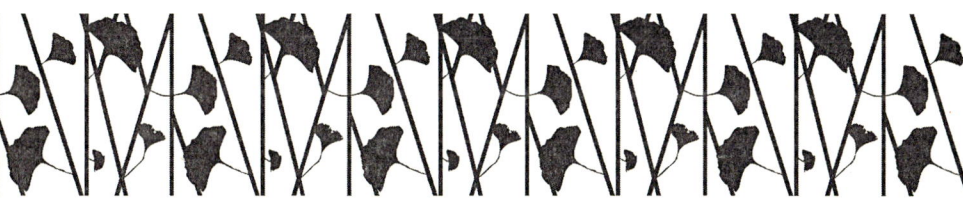

poems | George Looney

LOST HORSE PRESS
Sandpoint, Idaho

Cover Art: Oil painting, *Woman with a Lute,* by Johannes Vermeer.
Author Photo: John Fontecchio.
Book & Cover Design: Christine Holbert.

FIRST EDITION

This and other fine LOST HORSE PRESS titles may be viewed online at www.losthorsepress.org.

LIBRARY OF CONGRESS CATALOGING-IN-PUBLICATION DATA

Looney, George.
[Poems. Selections]
Meditations before the windows fail : poems / George Looney.—First edition.
     pages ; cm
ISBN 978-0-9908193-4-9 (softcover : acid-free paper)
I. Title.
PS3562.O597A6 2015
811'.54—dc23
                         2015020538

for Ohio, always, & in memory

CONTENTS

1   A Failed Translation of the World

3   Where Light Is Muted & Urgent

4   The Scent of a Lover's Flesh

5   Without Grace, Out of the Sky

6   What This Fog Would Have Us Believe

7   This Innocent Arrangement

8   The Beauty of Music Doesn't Have to Be Human

9   The Road Humming a Sinatra Tune

11   The Music of Stillness

12   The Glare Off These Panes

13   Ode to a Lover's Lips

14   Something Whimsical with Light

15   The Opposite of Love

16   Ode in Someone Else's Voice

17   Between the Touch of One Lover & the Touch of Another

18   To Kneel or Get Up Off Our Duffs

19   Unresolved Equations

20   Whispered Across a Flat State

21   The Sky Might As Well Be a Priest

22   Instruments to Accompany the Moon

23   Different Inebriations

24   An Invisible Violin with Perfect Pitch

26   Names Written in the Fog of Windows

27   Unmistakable Omens

28   Meditation at Night on a Lover in Another State

29   Out of Jukeboxes & Car Radios

30   Ruminations on a Sky Empty of Gulls

31   Maddened by Longing

32   A Sky Seamless with Clouds

33   As Simple as Math & Gravity

34   The Snow's Repertoire

35   What Voices Carry Miles

36   A Treatise on Our Need to Be Healed

37   Whatever Light Needs to Be Forgiven Of

38   The Hieroglyph of the Horizon

39   To Hell with the Deconstructionists

40   Snow Globes & Theories of Breakage

41   A Billboard Plastered with Hands

42   Assaying the Sky

43   Jukebox Snow Angels

45   A Guileless Moon, Whispering

46   Sad on Poles in the Midst of Fields

47   The Music of a Woman's Spine

48   Off the Hook

49   Every Song on the Radio Sad

50   A Tarantella of White & Wind

51   In Confusion, a Kind of Grace

52   Release, Our Sentence

53   First Victim of Not Enough Light

54   Meditation on a Sky Preparing to Snow

55   In the Form of an Opera by Mozart

And then the Windows failed—and then
I could not see to see.

—*Emily Dickinson*

A FAILED TRANSLATION OF THE WORLD

To begin with, this sky
doesn't have a clue & can't be said
to clearly predict what's coming.

Filtered through clouds gray enough
to seem wise, this light says

art is a failed translation
of how the world is. A room

in a hotel in a landscape flat enough
wind never slows
enough to catch its breath,

the drapes shut, ignores
what's coming down outside

& lets lovers lie, worn out
& damp, on a bed out of whack
with its frame enough to be

said to be aslant, or askew.
That is, if someone other
than the lovers were to walk in,

cursing what was coming down
outside & stop in mid-curse,

having come to the conclusion
it's not their room. The world is
off enough to allow for anything.

Distance always has the last word,
though. The lovers
always knew it was coming.

Snow comes down, formlessness
rounding off the edges
of what we had assumed was

reliable. The chaos within
the body longs for touch,
for the differentiated passion

of one body holding another
in a room where light is
muted *&* urgent *&* the air

is too warm to allow for
the expansiveness coming down
outside, where temperature

evokes the desire to remember
how it feels to fill
someone else's lungs with breath.

THE SCENT OF A LOVER'S FLESH

Calm, someone might say of this sky.
It's gone calm.

The branches of this oak
scraping it, calm

isn't the word that comes to mind,
the weathered American flag

a clear indicator of
a distinct absence of calm.

Everything's up in the air, & nothing
that's being said comes close

enough to the scent of a lover's
flesh to clarify direction, or distance.

To taste a lover's body is enough
to make us go anywhere, even calm.

WITHOUT GRACE, OUT OF THE SKY

The sky vacillates. No one remembers it
taking a stand on anything.
Any light is temporary, as you

could call the gulls who glide, music-less
& yet not without grace,
out of the sky to settle on lamp posts.

In northwest Ohio, the Black Swamp
rises, as gas, & makes
snow mime how a man & woman

dance, naked, in a hotel room, risen
from a bed damp with sex, believing
touch negates every argument.

This fog argues, with everything
cloaked in its gray, everything is

related, *&* very little is
authentic. Clouds gone to ground

tend to give credence to uncertainty.
Rumors thrive in what is

mere atmospherics, *&* the past
gets muddled enough to be left

standing on the wrong mark, having
missed its cue, not knowing what to say.

Despite what fog would have us believe,
touch is sacred, even as memory.

THIS INNOCENT ARRANGEMENT

The sky's weary. How much of
the world is
what we let loose on it?

Are we a plague the world needs
to fight off? A gull
dives a long, elaborate dance

the sky has to acknowledge
as a kind of joy in being

trapped in flesh & free
to dive through it
& let this innocent arrangement

of light & moisture & forces
we name but don't
understand take on what is

inside us, for better or worse.

THE BEAUTY OF MUSIC
DOESN'T HAVE TO BE HUMAN

This evening sky's a bruise.
Too often, in
trying to hold the world

we harm it. Given that,
I still want
these gulls not to

give up their chorus of sounds
that add to the music
the sky hums, an aria

no human throat could
mimic. I want to
read this tree's bare branches

like any text, all language
a longing for what is
being said that can't

ever be said. Tonight,
may this battered sky
hum more than one lullaby.

THE ROAD HUMMING A SINATRA TUNE

It's that point beyond which we know darkness
is all that's possible.

Light, they say, fades. They have it wrong.
Light ignores what folks whisper

& dons a leather jacket like James Dean wore
around the bend into oblivion,

lights up a cigarette from the pack
next to his heart,

takes a drag & lets loose a cloud
that gauzes his face. Light has had it

with all the stodgy rules folks want
him to live by. The road is humming

a Sinatra tune he can almost remember
the lyrics to. Whistling,

Light revs his engine & looks back
to see you, almost naked

in the doorway. Light slips on his shades
& you see yourself, small & delicate,

reflected in them. You find yourself
humming the Sinatra tune Light whistles.

You climb on the back of his bike
& press yourself into Light

& everything blurs with speed,
the dark something you refuse to imagine.

It's the kind of sky that used to be
compared to a lid.

Locked in, the skeletons of trees
dance in a wind that insists

nothing's alone. A feeble-minded bird
fights the wind. I want to

dance with a lover in some hotel room
close enough to the highway

rushing cars would provide all the music
we'd need. Love, let's move slower,

slow enough the skeletons of
trees would envy our grace.

Slow enough a witless bird might take us
for statues, & settle on us.

They must be the ghosts of gulls,
these flashes, peripheral,
of almost light. Perhaps longing

lures them to this window,
& the sorrow that comes with it
scares them off. The sky,

calm for once, is a miasma
of distance & some threat
not carried out. Ghosts of

gulls strafe this window,
playful, intoxicated
by the pleasure of swooping

& careening. The way, in memory,
a lover's lips move,
without sound, furtive, calming.

ODE TO A LOVER'S LIPS

for Ruth Ann

The sky, today, is blind with clouds,
the only birds vague, unnameable.

Wrapped in this numb shroud of light,
I remember a dim hotel room

& a lover's lips that could have uttered
the words to bring back the dead.

It's all in the manner of saying.
Those lips could have kissed this sky clear.

Nothing funny about a sky like this.
Crows, though, could be

laughing, the joke private & on us.
Memory's at risk, light a blur

we'd have to say is indistinct
at best. A chuckle

might be possible, if a cloud
did something whimsical with light.

And in dim hotel rooms, lovers
laugh at the silly positions

they sometimes find themselves in, passion
a mystery often comic.

THE OPPOSITE OF LOVE

Someone must have untied the ropes
that held fast the sky.

Released, it wants to rub light's shoulders
& press its lips to
the nape of her neck, under the hair

where her scent congregates.
The sky believes
breathing in the light's perfume

will help it live with the regret it can't
shake off, left every night,
alone, longing for the morning.

Light has another lover,
the sky figures, & doesn't know
how to choose. The sky

will never try to make light stay,
afraid of losing
the temporary pleasure of her smile.

To hold someone too tight
is the opposite of love.

To hold no one every night
is an ache
all the stars can't soothe.

This sky reminds me how difficult it is
to praise anything that moves us

& not have that praise turn maudlin
or end up ravaged & broke in some alley,

the taste of emptiness in its mouth
as it mumbles hollow promises

& asks for a dollar to buy a Danish
& a cup of coffee. How we want

to look away & hurry past this
sorry reminder of what it means

to accept the inherent pleasures of this world
for what they are & not turn them into

something more *us* than *other*. We want
all praise to come back to us

& we'll sing someone else's lyrics
as if we had written them & don't care

how our voice changes them. To light
on a day like this, any subterfuge

seems silly & just not worth the effort.
I want to be able to sing, in the voice

of this light, of lovers, their tongues
writing odes on one another's flesh.

BETWEEN THE TOUCH OF ONE LOVER &
THE TOUCH OF ANOTHER

No expanse of sky, no matter how close
the thought of collapse, is enough

to allow for love. Distance is an abstraction.
Forget what lies between the touch

of one lover & the touch of another,
the dented, familiar signs seem to say.

Think about it enough, they whisper
& whistle a tune you'd swear you've heard

though you can't recall a single note
until the signs get you to whistle it,

*& you won't ever find that hotel room you remember
holding a lover in.* No matter

how many gulls thrash their sharpened bodies
through this sky, the memory of touch is

a map folded open to the road you need to be on
to get back to that room & that lover.

TO KNEEL OR GET UP OFF OUR DUFFS

This sky, edges crisp, understated,
seems a formality. Maybe it is
a suggestion we could choose to ignore.

If this sky were the ceiling of a ballroom
or a chapel, would we know

whether to kneel & pray
or get up off our duffs & dance?

Maybe a hotel room in Ohio could have
enough room, enough music,

to satisfy our urge to hold one another
& spin & twirl & dip, formal or free style,
with a grace no sky's ever had room for.

This tectonic sky compresses the world
down into a longing

for the small of a woman's back,
the scent of her neck after love.

Too often what passes for lyric is a sham,
some clever canard draped in a shroud
of irony & lust. And faith, itself

a whimpering victim of too much pressure given in to
too readily, forgets the flesh
can't be ignored. To reason without the body

guarantees the equation won't be resolved
to anyone's satisfaction. This sky
can't keep me from remembering how

a woman's lips once convinced me
the world remains worth trying to say.

Folks here say the moon was whispered by a woman
who wanted her words to make it to a man
whose sorrow was a face turned away from the world.

They say the moon, the woman's whispered *Goodnight*,
drifted across a sky it fell in love with
&, by the time it got to the man, it wasn't a whisper

but the sky's pale & distant lover. Still, the man
looked up at the moon's face reflecting the sun
on the other side of the world & knew it was

the woman's voice set aloft to comfort him,
& blew it a kiss to send it back to
the woman whose throat had mothered its grace.

THE SKY MIGHT AS WELL BE A PRIEST

Last night the moon was a scythe
low in the sky & so beautiful

death, glimpsing itself in its orange blade,
smiled & took the night off.

This morning, the memory
of that blade of a moon
carves graffiti on my rough heart.

I want to swing the scythe that is memory
or the sliver of a moon

through the fields between here & Ohio
& cut down every weed

that grows despite the emptiness
in the language locals mumble

into a sky that might as well be a priest,
they confess so much to it.

There's nothing to keep me from
a hotel room & a woman
lovely enough to gather what's been cut

&, with it, weave together a man
who would shiver awake
in her arms, confess everything.

When we sleep our secret bodies come out
& do the tarantella or some fervent waltz.

They dance around us—ourselves re-imagined—
both our bodies & not our bodies.

They dance out into the world they've watched,
as if through a window, from within us,

& join up with the secret bodies of neighbors & friends
& lovers, the night one grand & elegant ballroom.

The moon serenades them with ballads of love,
& the earth, awake, tickles their bare feet

& plays its grasses & shrubs, exotic
string instruments to accompany the moon.

Not one of us, not one of them, thinks of
stopping till we wake & the dance is done.

My mother would've called this sky a character
& admonished it for distilling light

into something hard enough more than a shot or two
would set everything to spinning.

She'd have admitted it could sure clear the sinuses
though, & would've belted back a shot

before disappearing into the past, where,
still alive, she'll have a shot of gin before bed.

This sky, constructed of cirrus spires,
isn't so much a sky
as one of Calvino's invisible cities.

The women of this city
no one's ever been able to repeat the name of

do not walk, Marco Polo might have said,
they waltz, & the perpetual music
that defines the grace of their bodies

is the same music men hum in their sleep
& listen to in cars, the windows down,
admiring women dancing across the street

as they wait for the one red light to change
& then drive off, slow,

remembering women who are still in sight
& dancing to the music they listen to.

In this city that's not a sky, Marco
Polo sets down his maps & the Khan's atlas

& raises an invisible violin with perfect pitch
to his chin to stroke out a waltz

that keeps time with the women who dance
& make him weep for the loss
of every city he meant to make it to.

Marco Polo weeps & plays an invisible waltz,
knowing he'll never leave this unnamed city

where the very streets take up his music,
women out & waltzing everywhere.

Light this morning convinces what leaves are left
to slow dance as if violins
were wringing solace out of a music

that, given time & a horizon far enough off,
could get all the skeletons in any heart
up & swaying across a polished floor.

One car's parked alone at the end of the dance hall's lot.
Music the orchestra plays for the dancers
barely makes it to the couple coming back to their bodies

who write, with their fingers, their names
in the fog of the windows
& wrap them in a rough sign for the human heart.

If time were a cardinal, this sky would be enough
to drop it, a sudden heart attack,

the snow stained with the body of a bird
which is not a cardinal but time.

No one would mistake such scaled feet
for the first flowers of spring.

No matter how many images of the cardinal
flash through the camera
at speeds necessary for the illusion of depth,

no one would mistake it for a rose
& try to give it to a lover in a hotel room
as a sign of anything like passion.

MEDITATION AT NIGHT ON A LOVER
IN ANOTHER STATE

Dark out this window, clouds there
because too much is being lost

into the fickle emptiness between the stars
if they aren't. The clouds

would be gray with any light at all,
& remind us that being held,

if you're held in the right arms,
is the best any of us can hope for.

This sky has my number.
Not far off a siren wails,
the first Wednesday of the month.

This is a test, I know. That the sky has passed
the point of giving up
anything is a comfort, unexpected.

This light pretends the cold's a memory.
It isn't. And lovers aren't
picky about time, which is, after

all, an odd fellow who hums tunes
no one can sing the words to,

though everyone swears the song is
one they've sung along with
as it came out of jukeboxes & car radios.

No music someone has slipped quarters into
a slot to hear could be mistaken
by anyone for any kind of siren.

But it could be a warning to lovers
to hang on. That flesh is
the only redemption possible

in this world. That the tongues
of lovers have to tease
what meaning's possible from flesh.

Not even a single gull flying
to suggest the possibility of motion.

Light has assumed an alias
& scuttles through alleys,
mumbling in a gruff voice not its own.

No disguise is perfect. Sooner or later,
someone will shout its real name
& all bets will be off.

A gull shivers atop a lamp post,
burying its head in feathers
that, any other day, would let it fly.

The future has been, in the past,
read in those feathers.

Now, we believe the future hasn't happened,
& so can't be read in feathers

or even in the stark patterns left by
lovers dancing barefoot in wet grass.

The moon, a faint copy of itself,
hunkers in a late morning sky humming

a Sinatra ballad, trying not to
remember everyone has two sides.

No one knows the moon's other
pockmarked face, always
in the dark, that howls back

at coyotes & wolves & lovers
who, maddened by longing,
let out a cry that can be mistaken

for animal. It's a human desire,
one the moon knows well,

cursed, as it is, to circle the lover
it hides its dark side from.

Murders of crows in the trees
serenade the moon
with the tune it hums to itself

& someone hums, off key,
turning in the dark
to ask a lover the lyrics.

No amount of bravado can
disguise the foolishness
of arguing with what this sky offers.

It's the sort of gray that calms.
Whatever might come down,
don't worry. A lone gull,

with its stark, honed body,
cuts this elegant sky,
tailor's shears through the finest lace.

AS SIMPLE AS MATH & GRAVITY

Not even crows know what to say
to make everything go back
to how it once was. Time,

that out-of-work machinist
with hands burned raw
& a face with lines deep enough

to misplace a moon in,
won't give in to anything
as simple as math, & gravity

has a few choice words
time would choose, no doubt,
to ignore. The text being

laid down flake by flake
enhances light. Are there enough
words, in the snow,

to name every hue of light
reflected from the bodies of lovers?

With enough distance, the drift down of snow
signals a loss. Close up,

what's said about these crystals may be
true, each a singular expression

of longing. Think of every flake
as lips. What they sing,
accompanied by the low moan

of an acoustic guitar, is a ballad
that won't let you forget
what it can mean to hold a lover

in some hotel room, the world outside
gone white, faded into memory.

Memory isn't enough to bless
or condemn the light
this sky is saddled with.

To begin to translate this light
into language, remember
a night in a hotel room

in a terrain flat enough voices
carry miles. Pretend
your tongue made your lover

declare pleasure with a voice
almost another's. Imagine
it was enough, that crying out,

to make you believe the world
is a place joy is
not only possible, but probable.

If this were memory & not
imagining, your lover's taste
would still be on your lips.

This sky lies about time. Clouds
carve the lie into sentence fragments,

condensation in cahoots with this light.
Here is the time, Rilke said,

for the sayable. Maybe he was
wrong. Maybe he was taken in

by the lies of a sky as rigid
as this one. Maybe everything

that can be said can't come close
to the vocabulary of the slightest touch.

WHATEVER LIGHT NEEDS TO BE FORGIVEN OF

The confession this sky is
reminds me sorrow,
despite its claim on us,

isn't everything. There is
this blue that can't be pinned down

to one shade, & its insistence
it wants to go for drinks
& shoot pool. After,

drunk, it'll stagger out the bar
& slap me on the back.

Go home, it will say,
& hold your lover until distance is
forgotten. Forgive light

whatever it needs to be
forgiven of. Confession has
nothing on two bodies

naked & holding each other
on a bed where the sheets haven't had
time enough to dry.

Remember, it will say,
absolution comes best through the flesh.

This gauze of air winds around
men & women who walk through it
& leave their likenesses.

The past must be like this,
all faint after-images & denial.

Memory can't keep a body bandaged
& whole & warm. It is

a hieroglyph scrawled inside the body,
its lyric bird head
looking off to the horizon,

as if a rigid line could hold some solace
a body could breathe in & live off.

TO HELL WITH THE DECONSTRUCTIONISTS

Nothing about this sky suggests how to read it.
To be critical of light made spurious

by clouds seems petty *&* too predictable,
& any birds are too far off to be named.

Once the sky brokered a deal with the devil
& called itself a deluge

a man *&* woman rode out in some hotel room,
writing texts on one another with their tongues.

To hell with the deconstructionists.
The body was what they tasted *&* nothing more.

The lovers would have said they didn't need
any explanation, any other text.

The weather has broken, they say, meaning
the inevitable has happened.

Yesterday, I mucked through under a sky
curved in such a way I could imagine

someone might pick up this collapsed world
& shake it & start snow falling again.

Today, the sky a blue scar, it's hard to believe
any of this was ever that held in.

Still, lovers hold each other & don't
let go, hoping for any kind of break.

Luck isn't a concept this sky would stoop to
understand, or give in to. This wind,

brazen & all too sure of the inevitable,
whistles through fingers crossed as if an inane gesture
could determine the outcome of anything.

Crows sprawled in the branches of a dying oak
could be mistaken, from a distance,

for letters, shaky, as if the hand that scrawled them
had trembled from exposure
to cold & the memory of a hotel room

where fingers, warm, slipped into a lover's body
& the shivering that followed was enough

to make any sky an advertisement for gambling,
a billboard plastered with hands the size of condominiums
letting fly dice in search of numbers.

Nothing is so random as convincing
lovers holding one another

they have to let go, to give this up. Not even
the sky, with all its light, should
be able to do such a number on lovers.

Better they ignore the sky & its pale certainty.
Better they let passion determine the odds.

Not the sky again. Not this
gray advice to those
who would look up & believe

there's something there to see,
to listen to. The sky
doesn't have any answers.

Pleasure hunkers in the flesh,
the body the lonesome tip
of the iceberg that spends its time

out of the water. Ships have
gone down for mistaking
that sliver of ice for everything

there. They pray
at the bottom of cold seas—
victims who, stoic, ignored

what they must have been
told, in voices
sounding dire, was there.

Some days the sky is suffused with such light
it seems a disguise.

So we wonder, if everything's going
incognito, what we can trust.

The world flirts with us, it seems.
We want to know its intentions
& if the myth is true

in which the ragged & shivering treetops
scratch words into the illusion
of a sky near enough to write on.

We want to know what stories
have been scraped there.

Lovers, naked in a hotel room, want
to run, screaming, out the door

& roll in snow until their bodies steam
& run back in & make love again,
everything wet & passionate.

But that would mean leaving the bed
they've signed with their bodies,

wanton snow angels in misshapen sheets.
A faint music comes from
the next room, or their own mouths,

that soothes their bodies & lets them
sleep, believing that, when they wake,

their bodies will hum for days, the sky
a familiar love song coming out
of every radio & jukebox in the world.

A GUILELESS MOON, WHISPERING

This snow's a measure of speed & nothing
is safe. Not even a crow
would fly in this.

The guileless moon has whispered so
long crows fill trees
in good weather & bad.

What light there is only harasses those of us
trying not to be late
for the last train pulling out

down tracks buried under what comes down
in the delicate form of
an explosion of what *was* water.

To turn in the midst of such a storm
is to lose the way,
no matter how slow you might be moving.

It's always better to turn toward a lover
beside you in bed
who whispers your name

& makes a sound low in the throat
that could never be mistaken
for the caw of a moon-lured crow.

Crows slice through what light there is,
only the occasional wing beat

to indicate they're not some confusion
of shadow & light. They take on

the guise of the last remnants of curses
the gods flung down at a man & woman

holding one another in a familiar dark
& humming sentimental love songs.

Hearing the raucous caws, one of them
thinks of the practice of hanging figures,

stuffed with straw & dressed in unfashionable clothes,
sad, on poles in the midst of fields of corn.

Nothing scares crows in this sky. And memory,
the other thinks, strung up on a pole in some field,

will lose its shape as the straw falls out to form
obscure runes on frozen ground.

A skein of anonymous birds, small & dark,
wrings this gray sky taut,

a whirlwind of song I imagine through
this institutional window. Loneliness is

more than can be serenaded away
by mundane birds, no matter how many

twist together in a desperate ascension
riddled with wings & light.

The sky's an interrogation of clouds
any one of us might break under,

& nothing heals like touching the aria,
delicate, along the small of a woman's back.

No sky, no matter how addictive,
will convince me

anything I could say
could make this easier for anyone,

& the absence of gulls, or even sparrows,
denies me the chance to
make the sky an absolution.

Confession is an elixir meant to fix everything
that fixes nothing.

Whether this sky deserves to be described as empty
isn't my concern.

To be held in the arms of a lover,
even if it's not a cure,
would be a comfort

& would let everything off the hook
to be what it is, nothing more.

for Diane

Not even the thought of house sparrows
is a comfort. The feeble illumination from

a single lamp's not enough to suggest anything
other than just how little we can be sure of

when the sky's a roiling contrivance of clouds
dark enough to deny a gull safe passage.

Some days, memory isn't enough,
every song on the radio sad.

Somewhere, though, a woman sways,
just out of the shower,

her body, gleaming, the only light
that could save any world loss has hold of.

The music this sky hums could break
your heart. Don't let it. Dance

to the haunted & hallowed humming
the sky lays down like a hard truth
that could make every snowflake

follow a different pattern. Everything is
swirling, a passionate tarantella
of white & wind. Let your body, naked

in the maelstrom, twirl with such passion
no single eddy of fog & snow
could wrap you up or hold you for long.

Dance, love, & convince the sky
it shouldn't let go of music this pure.

This winter sky wants to hold everything in.
Desire has no greater advocate

than clouds pregnant with what must be
memory. To remember

the warmth of a lover's lips is to know
anything can be lost.

That desire is even possible on such a day,
under such clouds, means

prayer is more than wishing. It is
one way we hold on to what's cherished.

The sky let loose, all bets are off,
the game rigged, someone at a radar screen
pretending the edge of a front is

the curve of a woman's hip
he imagines tracing with his tongue

in some hotel room, curtains drawn
to forget what's coming down outside
where everything's released,

the world one long shiver, a low moan
of light coming from the one lamp post

close enough to the hotel room a woman,
shivering, might notice it
through where the curtains don't quite meet

& think it odd that this distant light
sings what sounds like a hymn

as she comes, the man's tongue
touching her to a music
that seems to match what she hears

the lamp post humming,
all one music the sky's let loose.

FIRST VICTIM OF NOT ENOUGH LIGHT

The sky today is a confluence of desire
& loss. As it is,
in different forms, every day.

Light is the font for the first time in weeks,
not the aggravation of clouds.

Here, where gray is so familiar
we know what the lines in its palms say
about the future, we're not sure

how to smile at a stranger or if we should,
trust the first victim of not enough light.

No sky can take the place of a lover.
Touch is the body giving in to trust.

Clouds carve this sky into longing.
Whatever lone birds feel
the need to hover in this wind off the lake

are commas that punctuate complex sentences
written to explain loss.

Before sunlight turns what leaves are left
into a waltz in three-quarter time,

these clouds will give up the memories they hold
& let them drift down,
white shards cold enough to slice a heart.

IN THE FORM OF AN OPERA BY MOZART

This white-out of snow is the rumor of an aria
in an unknown opera by Mozart.

The first scene opens on what seems to be
a hotel room, the curtains drawn, only one lamp on.
The room has the feel of expectation.

A solitary violin begins playing
what will be this opera's theme.

A man holds a woman as if she were memory.
They dance, not to the violin's quaint music

but to an orchestra out of the past
that lures the moon out of the sky to listen.

Later, the woman straddling the man in bed,
the wind instruments & the brass
have their various ways with the theme.

Their bodies follow the music's lead.
Outside, the world is missing.
The lovers collapse into one another.

After, the man takes the violin to his chin
& plays the theme from the opening scene,
the music that's been here all along.

ACKNOWLEDGMENTS

The following poems were first published in the journals cited. The author is grateful to the editors of these journals for first giving these poems a place.

The Laurel Review: "A Failed Translation of the World," "Out of Jukeboxes & Car Radios" and "Whatever Light Needs to Be Forgiven of"

The Chaffey Review: "Without Grace, Out of the Sky," "The Road Humming a Sinatra Tune," and "As Simple as Math & Gravity"

The Kerf: "What This Fog Would Have Us Believe," "The Music of Stillness" (as "Music Out of a Fervent Wind"), "Names Written in the Fog of Windows" (as "What the Sky Would Like to Claim"), "Ruminations on a Sky Empty of Gulls," and "The Snow's Repertoire"

The Florida Review: "This Innocent Arrangement" and "A Tarantella of White & Wind"

Bellevue Literary Journal: "The Beauty of Music Doesn't Have to Be Human"

Cimarron Review: "The Opposite of Love"

Third Coast: "Ode in Someone Else's Voice"

Redivider: "Between the Touch of One Lover & the Touch of Another"

The Chariton Review: "Unresolved Equations"

The Journal: "The Sky Might as Well Be a Priest"

Whiskey Island Magazine: "Instruments to Accompany the Moon," "Snow Globes & Theories of Breakage," and "A Billboard Plastered with Hands"

The Southern Review: "An Invisible Violin with Perfect Pitch"

Two Rivers Review: "Meditation at Night on a Woman in Another State"

American Literary Review: "Maddened by Longing" and "Off the Hook"

Minnetonka Review: "The Hieroglyph of the Horizon"

Bayou Magazine: "To Hell With the Deconstructionists"

Eclipse: "Assaying the Sky" and "A Guileless Moon, Whispering"

Blueline: "Sad on Poles in the Midst of Fields"

Puerto del Sol: "Jukebox Snow Angels"

Great River Review: "The Music of a Woman's Spine"

The Louisville Review: "Every Song on the Radio Sad"

Bateau: "Release, Our Sentence"

The Chaffin Journal: "Meditation on a Sky Beginning to Snow"

The editors of *Bellevue Literary Journal* nominated "The Beauty of Music Doesn't Have to Be Human" for a Pushcart Prize.

GEORGE LOONEY's books include a book-length poem, *Structures the Wind Sings Through* (2014), *Monks Beginning to Waltz* (2012), *A Short Bestiary of Love and Madness* (2011), *Open Between Us* (2010), *The Precarious Rhetoric of Angels* (2005), *Attendant Ghosts* (2000), *Animals Housed in the Pleasure of Flesh* (1995), and the novella *Hymn of Ash* (2008). He founded the BFA in Creative Writing Program at Penn State Erie and serves as editor-in-chief of the international literary journal *Lake Effect*, translation editor of *Mid-American Review*, and he is a co-founder of the Chautauqua Writers' Festival.